20 Little Piano Pieces from Around the World

by David Patterson

Illustrations by TenBroeck Davison

Cover illustration by Ellen Appleby

ED 4066

First Printing: September 1998

ISBN - 978-0-7935-9157-2

G. SCHIRMER, Inc.

DISTRIBUTED BY

HAL•LEONARD®
CORPORATION
7777 W. BLUEMOUND RD. P.O. BOX 13819 MILWAUKEE, WI 53213

CONTENTS

20 Little Piano Pieces from Around the World serves as a study in basic technique for the beginning pianist—of any age—and as an introduction to music from around the world.

Appearing in virtually every conceivable size and shape for every imaginable use, musical instruments are the expressive voices of the world's peoples. Throughout history, music has played a central role in the rituals and the imagination of communities everywhere. Isaiah, poet and prophet, describes two of nature's own instruments:

> the mountains and the hills break forth into singing . . . and all the trees of the
> fields clap their hands.

Since ancient times, the Acoma have sung and played their musical instruments—drums, rattles, and bells—in their pueblo known as the "Sky City," which sits atop a mesa rising 400 feet above the central New Mexico plains. The Acoma have no word for "music." That which comes closest to describing music is *haastu*, feast or celebration. For these people, as in many other cultures, celebration and music are inseparable.

In this collection we have gathered and adapted twenty traditional songs and dances from six continents, along with translations and information about the music and the people who perform it. There are illustrations of some of the instruments associated with the music, and we've included a guide to assist in the pronunciation of difficult words. To allow for preferences of student and teacher, fingerings have been omitted.

—DAVID PATTERSON

ABOUT THE AUTHOR AND ILLUSTRATOR

David Patterson holds a doctorate from Harvard University and is on the faculty of the University of Massachusetts. He has taught for many years an international body of students with whom the exchange of music and ideas continues in earnest. TenBroeck Davison is an advocate of the arts and a lyricist who has written about life along the Texas border.

Their work in this collection is based largely on primary sources, which include interviews with native musicians and the research of Franz Boas (Eskimo music), Virginia Giglio (Cheyenne songs), M. de Laborde (Icelandic tradition), Francis O'Neill (Irish music), Colin McPhee (Balinese gamelan), and V.N. Bhatkhande (Indian ragas), among others.

"Neh́ minst" is an excerpt from *Southern Cheyenne Women's Songs* by Virginia Giglio (University of Oklahoma Press, 1994). Used by arrangement with University of Oklahoma Press.

"Gamelan" is taken from "Taboeh Teloe," transcribed for two pianos by Colin McPhee in his *Balinese Ceremonial Music* (G. Schirmer, Inc., 1940).

1. Qaggi

Nettilling ([The Lake] with Seals)

Canada

Translation: Tomorrow we begin pulling toward the northwest, up the country, *ija jija aja a.* (*Inuit*)

Qaggi means singing house built out of snow by the Inuit, or Eskimo, from Nunavut in the Northwest Territories of Canada. During winter, everyone in the village gathers in this singing house to celebrate feasts. They stand around a pillar of snow in the center of the main room where lamps are placed. There is singing, dancing, and playing of the drum (*kilaut*) made from the skin of a deer or seal which has been stretched over a hoop made from wood or from the fin of a whale. The voice and drum are the Inuit's only instruments, probably because they are always moving and cannot carry many possessions with them on their travels.

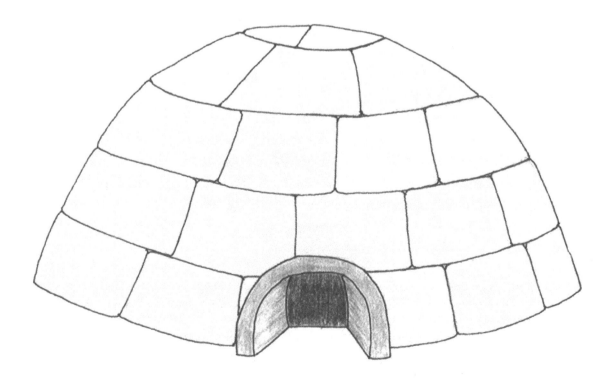

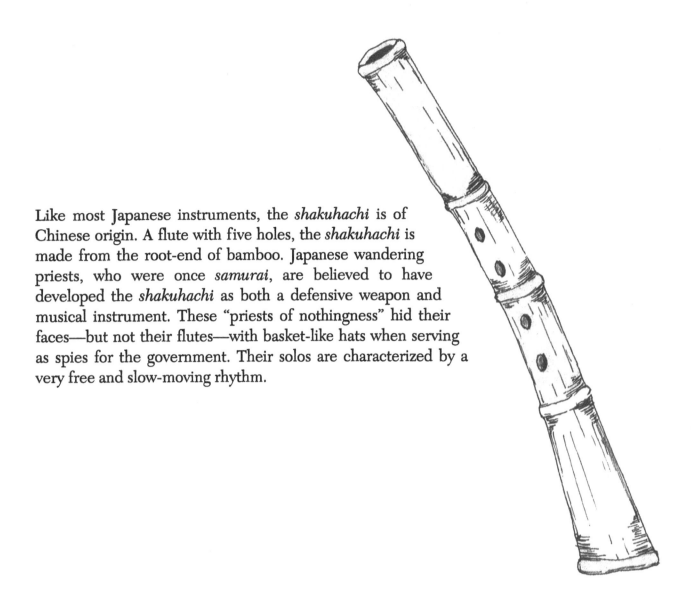

Like most Japanese instruments, the *shakuhachi* is of Chinese origin. A flute with five holes, the *shakuhachi* is made from the root-end of bamboo. Japanese wandering priests, who were once *samurai*, are believed to have developed the *shakuhachi* as both a defensive weapon and musical instrument. These "priests of nothingness" hid their faces—but not their flutes—with basket-like hats when serving as spies for the government. Their solos are characterized by a very free and slow-moving rhythm.

2. Shakuhachi

Choshi (Short Prelude)   Japan

3. Ch'in

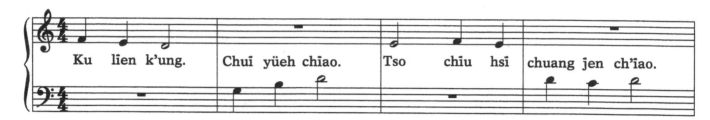

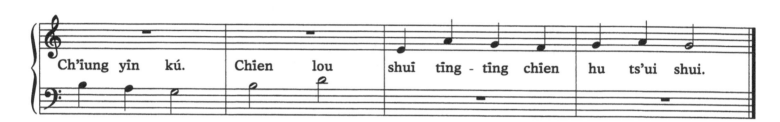

Ku lien k'ung. Chui yüeh chiao. Tso chiu hsi chuang jen ch'iao.

Ch'iung yin kú. Chien lou shui ting - ting chien hu ts'ui shui.

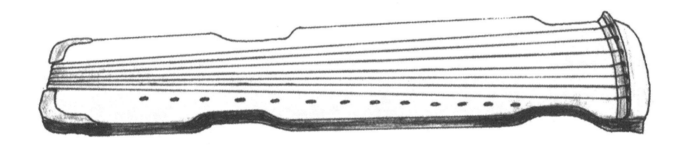

Translation: The old bamboo curtain makes the room feel empty. The moon shines brightly. People are sitting sadly by the window and waiting. It seems that the cricket also sings of sorrow. Water-drops ting ting, slowly. The pot of [soldier's] arrows makes the morning come sooner. *Chiang K'uei, poet and musician of the Sung Dynasty (1127–1278). (Mandarin)*

The *ch'in* is a long zither whose features correspond to the universe. The length of the instrument measures 3.65 "Chinese feet," for the 365 days of the year. A round upper board symbolizes heaven. A flat lower board with two openings—the dragon pond and phoenix pool—symbolizes earth. Thirteen inlaid discs to guide the fingers in playing represent the moons. Seven silk strings stand for emperors and mandarins. The *ch'in* (15th century B.C.) remains to this day one of the most ancient and honored Chinese instruments.

4. Mbira

Nyamaropa (Ancient Battle Chant)

Africa

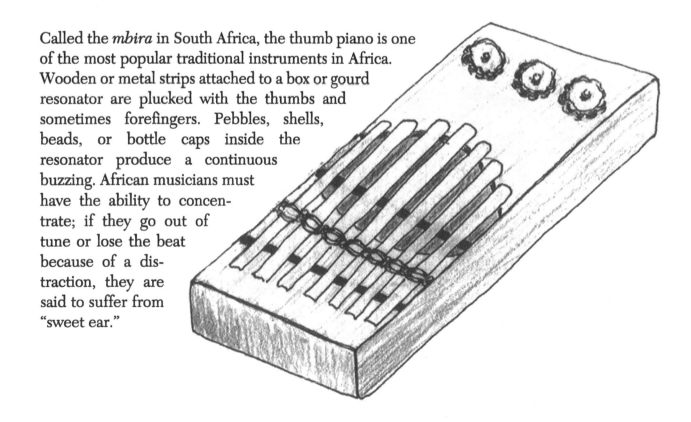

Called the *mbira* in South Africa, the thumb piano is one of the most popular traditional instruments in Africa. Wooden or metal strips attached to a box or gourd resonator are plucked with the thumbs and sometimes forefingers. Pebbles, shells, beads, or bottle caps inside the resonator produce a continuous buzzing. African musicians must have the ability to concentrate; if they go out of tune or lose the beat because of a distraction, they are said to suffer from "sweet ear."

5. Bells

Bob Doubles England

(2)   (1)   (4)   (3)   (5)

21435
24153
42513
45231
54321

These are the first five changes to the method of change ringing called "Bob Doubles."

A methodical way of playing tower *bells* in England is called ringing the changes. In the method "Bob Doubles," a peal for five *bells*, there are 120 different changes—orders—of the numbers 12345 (5 x 4 x 3 x 2 x 1 = 120). When there are as many as 10 *bells*, only some of the 3,628,800 possible changes are rung. Nowadays, change ringing has been taken up by handbell choirs.

Neĥ minst means "soft song," or lullaby, in Southern Cheyenne (*mo-minst* in Northern Cheyenne). Plains Indians, the Cheyennes believe that some songs come to them from the supernatural world through visions while others are borrowed from neighboring tribes. This lullaby, with "words" that have no known meaning, is sung over and over until the baby falls to sleep.

6. Neĥ minst

Bertha Little Coyote's Lullaby  North America

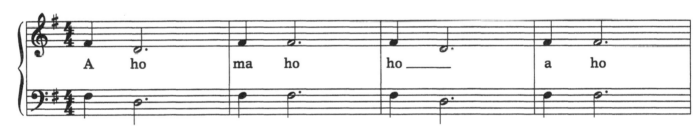

A ho ma ho ho _____ a ho

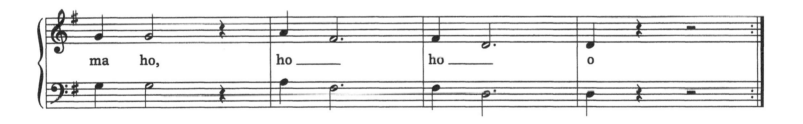

ma ho, ho _____ ho _____ o

7. Đàn Bầu

Chim Quyên (Lovebirds)   Vietnam

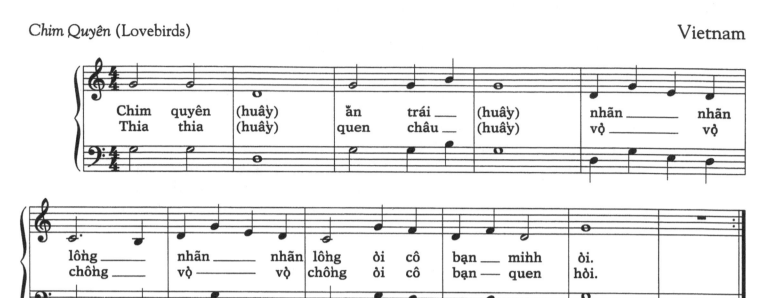

Chim   quyên   (huây)   ăn   trái ___   (huây)   nhãn ___   nhãn
Thia   thia   (huây)   quen châu ___   (huây)   vọ ___   vọ

lông ___   nhãn ___   nhãn lông òi   cô   bạn ___ mình   òi.
chông ___   vọ ___   vọ   chông òi   cô   bạn ___ quen   hỏi.

Translation: The lovebirds and the longan fruit, the fish and the lake. We, husband and wife, cannot forget each other's scent, even when we are apart. (*Vietnamese*)

Background: The expression *huây* does not belong to the poem, but is added to tell us that this song comes from the south country. It is the custom in Vietnam to gift every bride and groom with a pillow whose decoration is a heart flanked by two lovebirds.

This single-string box zither is of Vietnamese origin, one of very few Vietnamese instruments not from China. *Đàn* means instrument and *bầu* means gourd. The narrow instrument rests lengthwise on a stand. Attached vertically at one end of its string is a bamboo stem, or tuning stick. When the player plucks the string with one hand and, with the other, moves the stick in different directions, the pitch rises and falls. If the stick is moved slowly, a sliding tone is created; if quickly, the result is a vibrato. According to Vietnamese legend, a fairy created this "singing" instrument for a blind woman.

8. Làngspil

Lilja (Lily)

Fy - rri menn at frae - din _ Kun - no Forn ok klok a - hei-dnum Bò-kum,

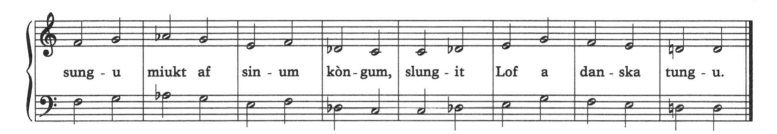

sung - u miukt af sin - um kòn-gum, slung - it Lof a dan - ska tung - u.

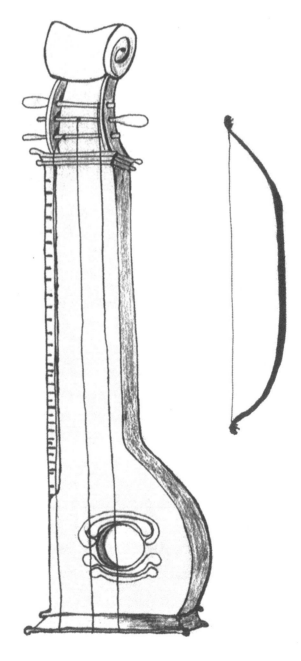

Translation: They will possess the highest knowledge, written with such elegance as that found in the most ancient books of sovereigns. They will sing in their Danish verse the praises of the princes. *Eystein Asgrimsson, poet, died 1361.* (*Old Norse*)

Background: The melody is called "Lily." These words are from a long poem dating back to about the time of the Vikings who settled in Iceland over 1,000 years ago. There is an old Icelandic saying, "every poet would have liked to have written this poem."

Little is known about the *làngspil*, one of very few musical instruments from Iceland. Some evidence indicates that it was played in the 19th century and possibly even earlier. On the verge of extinction, the *làngspil* has recently attracted the attention of Icelanders anxious to preserve their musical tradition. Resembling the Norwegian *làngeleik* ("long instrument"), the *làngspil* is a bowed box zither with one to six strings. It is played on a table or on a board placed across the knees.

Translation: Two youths go and come, *ha laleh djan laleh*. (*Eastern Armenian dialect*)

A double reed instrument with nine holes is known as the *duduk* in the Caucasus—Armenia, Azerbaijan, and Georgia. Always made from wood of the apricot tree, *Prunus armeniaca* (native to west Asia and cultivated for a long time in Armenia), the *duduk* sounds like no other instrument. *Duduks* are played in pairs, one performer improvising a melody and the other sustaining a drone on the tonic note. The melodies may be slow and songful, fast and dance-like, or they may move freely in time without any beat.

9. Duduk

Mokats Shuken (The Market at Mōk)   The Caucasus

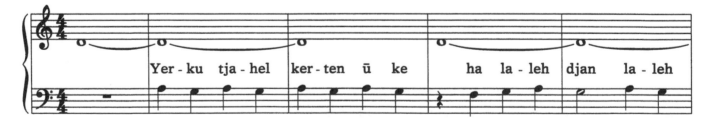

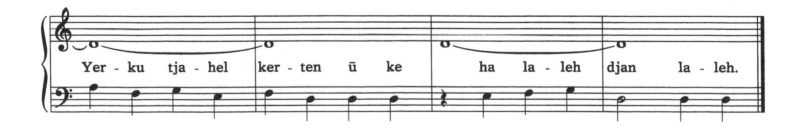

Background: The two words of this song, *mabelala mandya* (in the shallow sea), are in the *Enindilyagwa* language.

For centuries, the only instruments played by the aborigines of northern Australia have been the rhythm sticks, the boomerang, and the *didjeridu*. A natural trumpet, the *didjeridu* is a eucalyptus branch of up to six feet long hollowed out by termites. Using circular breathing (through the nose), the musician sustains a low drone embellished with rhythmic or timbral variations— always as accompaniment to a singer who marks the rhythm with either sticks or a boomerang.

10. Didjeridu

Mabelala Mandya ([Shark] in the Shallow Sea)

Australia

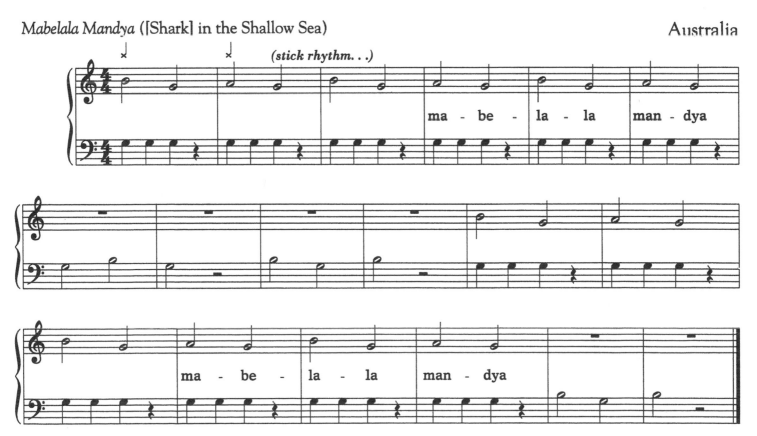

11. Jug Band

Such a Gittin' Upstairs   United States

De po-ny rar'd, de po-ny pitch'd, throwed ole mis-sus in de ditch. Such a

whooo   whooo   whooo   whooo   whooo   whooo

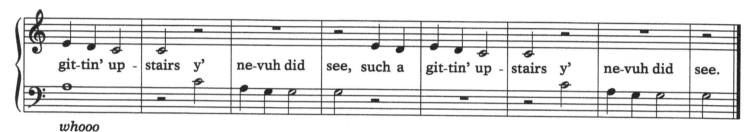

git-tin' up-stairs y' ne-vuh did see, such a git-tin' up-stairs y' ne-vuh did see.

whooo

Background: Children of slaves found themselves in trouble were they to be seen or heard laughing at any member of the plantation owner's family.

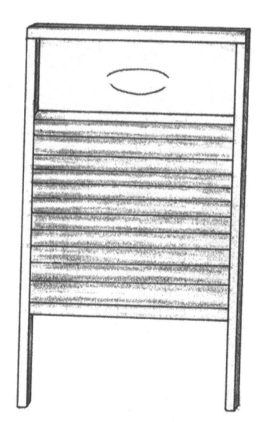

The *jug band* of the southern United States is named after its bass instrument, the jug, on which a player could produce one or two—possibly three—notes at most. The harmonica, banjo, washboard, kazoo, comb, and the washtub bass (with clothesline for the string) added to the band's unusual sound. *Jug bands* played on street corners and plantations, giving their renditions of the blues and songs of bondage.

A *klezmer* is a Jewish musician originally from Eastern European communities and German ghettos. *Klezmer* is a Yiddish word made up of two Hebrew words, *keley* and *zemer*, meaning musical instruments. An ensemble of *klezmorim* often features the clarinet, accompanied by accordion, double bass, and drums. Such an ensemble can be found playing at festive occasions, especially weddings and dances.

12. Klezmer

Freilach (Yiddish Dance)   Eastern Europe

13. Irish Fiddle

Dublin Streets   Ireland

The *Irish fiddle* and the European violin are one and the same instrument. Fiddlers say that if there is a difference between the two it is the price! This may be one reason so many musicians prefer the fiddle over other traditional Irish instruments. Other reasons might be because the fiddle is more portable than the harp and less finicky than the *uilleann*, or "the pipes" (both are names for the Irish bagpipe). Even the tin whistle has taken a back seat to the *Irish fiddle*.

Translation: *Señora Chichera* sell me some corn beer. If you don't have any, just whatever . . . some popcorn. (*Spanish*)

Background: References to corn appear throughout the music and mythology of many South American countries. The word *palomita* literally means dove, whose shape and color resemble a kernel of popped corn.

The *siku* comes from the Andean region of Bolivia, Chile, and Peru. A panpipe, the *siku* has not one, but two rows of bamboo pipes arranged according to length in a pattern that resembles a staircase. Pebbles are placed inside a pipe to raise its pitch. Since there are not enough pipes on one *siku* to cover the range of notes in an entire melody, two or more instruments are needed. Trading notes of the melody back and forth between performers causes an overlapping effect that is at once rhythmic and colorful.

14. Siku

Señora Chichera

South America

Se - ño - ra Chi - che - ra ven - de - me chi - chi - ta.

Si no tie - ne chi - cha, cual - quier co - si - ta... u - na pa - lo - mi - ta.

15. Sitār and Tamburā

Background: The names of the notes of the Indian scale are frequently used in the singing of a raga. This raga is performed in the morning; its mood is one of dignity.

sa ri ga ma pa dha ni sa (do re mi fa sol la ti do)

From northern India come two long-necked lutes, the *sitār*, with seven principal strings, and the *tamburā*, with only four strings. The *sitār* carries the melody, or raga, and is always accompanied by the *tamburā*, which supplies a drone centered on *sa*, the first note of the Indian scale. Both players sit on the floor, cross-legged. Magic, moods, and musical theory are closely linked to the tradition of performing ragas at certain times of the day or night, or during a particular season.

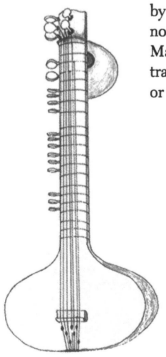

16. Gamelan

Tabu talōh (Gamelan Overture)

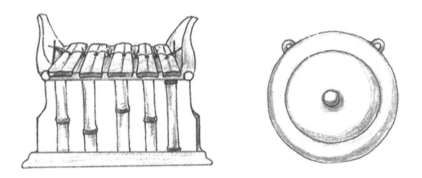

An orchestra from the Indonesian islands of Java and Bali, the *gamelan* features the sounds of bronze and iron in xylophone-like instruments, tuned gongs, gong-chimes, and cymbals. The sonorous Javanese *gamelan* contrasts the brilliant Balinese *gamelan*. *Ding, dong, deng, dung, dang* are the names for E F G B C, which form the most popular scale used in Balinese festival music.

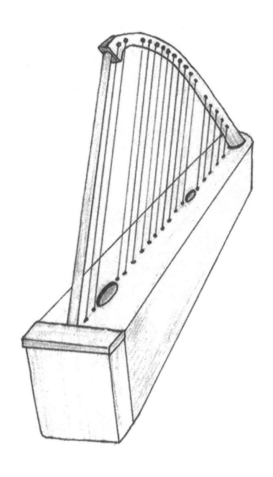

17. Arpa

Cuera Mohelam (Old Music Strings)   Mexico

The Yaqui Indians of northwestern Mexico and, more recently, Arizona and New Mexico, play the *arpa*, or harp, in fiestas that begin at sundown and continue until dawn. Of Spanish influence, the instrument has a large box resonator and simple appearance. It can be heard in dances and songs about the ancient Yaqui flower world called *seyewailo*. The music describes the beauty of flowers and the magic of the flower world.

18. 'Ūd

Ilim Ilim (Knowledge)

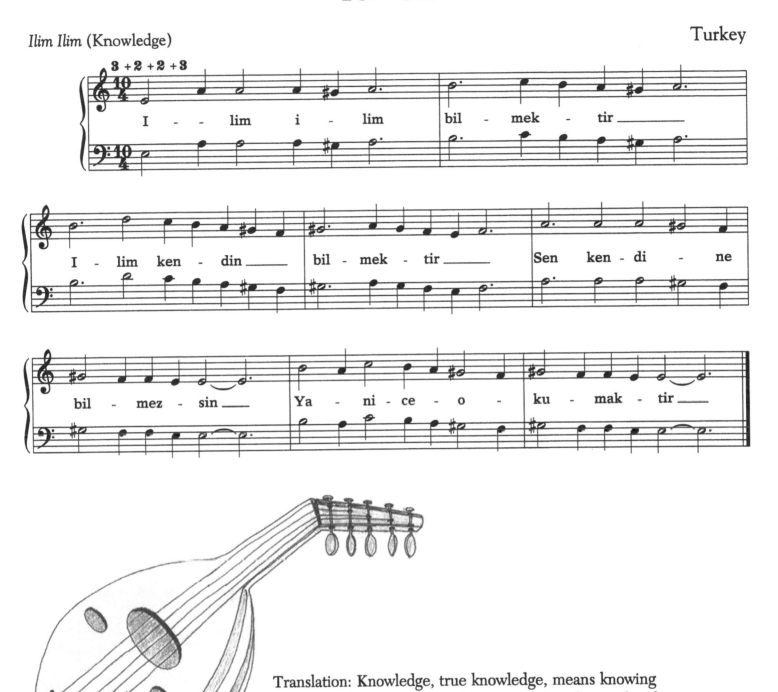

I - lim i - lim bil - mek - tir

I - lim ken - din bil - mek - tir Sen ken - di - ne

bil - mez - sin Ya - ni - ce - o - ku - mak - tir

Translation: Knowledge, true knowledge, means knowing yourself. Indeed, reading and learning are only worthy if you understand yourself, heart and soul. *Yunis Emre, poet, died 1320? (Turkish)*

For centuries the *'ūd*, a short-necked lute, has been the most played instrument in Arab countries from Egypt to Iraq. *'Ūd* means wood. The European name, lute, is derived from its Arabic forerunner, *al 'ūd*. The original four strings symbolized bile, blood, phlegm, and black bile. A fifth string was added to represent the soul. Early on, the strings were plucked with the quill of an eagle feather.

19. Guitarra

Background: *Soleares* comes from the Spanish word *soledad*, meaning loneliness. Aficionados say that *Soleares* is the "mother" of flamenco.

The *guitarra* from Andalucía in southern Spain is lighter and somewhat smaller than a classical guitar. It is designed for flamenco music, a music possibly from Arabic-speaking peoples to the south, Gypsies to the east and north, and local Andalusian folk. Flamenco comprises "deep" song, dance with foot-stamping and finger-snapping, and guitar-playing. The term *duende* (spirit) describes the state of musical ecstasy that both performer and listener may attain through flamenco art.

20. Umthuthuzelo

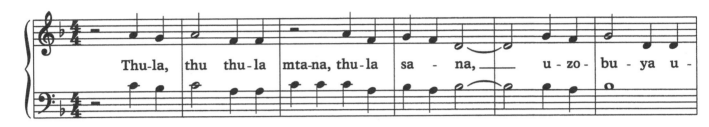

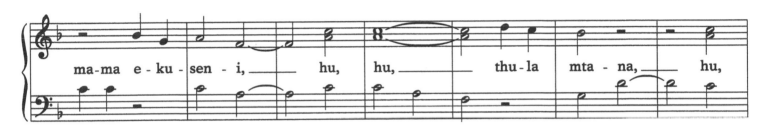

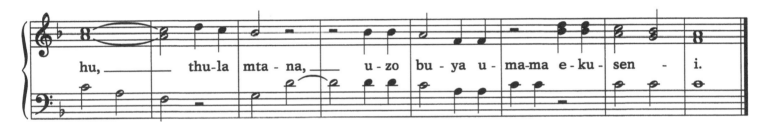

Translation: Silent, silent child, silent son, your mother will be back in the morning, *hoo, hoo.* (*Zulu*)

Music comes from deep in the hearts of the South African people. They cannot "begin" a song, because it existed before they were born. They cannot "end" a song, because it will continue long after they die—that is why one song may cross over into another or may simply fade away for the time being. The noun *umthuthuzelo* means comforting a child and is one of many different ways of saying lullaby.

PRONUNCIATION GUIDE

Vowels are usually pronounced as in Italian or Spanish:

a	as in father
e	as in red
i	as in pita
o	as in old
u	as in rule

Consonants are usually pronounced as in English, but always roll the "r" and always pronounce "th" like a hard "t."

SPECIAL CASES:

3. Ch'in

hs	sh as in ship
j	r as in run

7. Đàn Bâù

bạn	as in fan
huẫy	way
mỉnh	mon as in Monday
nhãn	nyen
ô	as in long
quen	when
quyên	kin
vỏ	vah

8. Làngspil

à	ow as in how
ae	i as in ride
ei, i	i as in sit
j	y as in yes
o	aw as in law
ò	o as in old
u	French *eu* as in *deux*
u when followed by k, ng, nk	u as in rule

9. Duduk

dj	j as in jar
tj	ch as in chop

18. 'Ūd

a	u as in fun
c	j as in jar
i	i as in sit
o	o as in stop
u	u as in full